Level 1 • Book 1

Themes

I Think I Can

Away We Grow!

SRA Imagine It!

Level 1 Book 1

Program Authors

Carl Bereiter

Andy Biemiller

Joe Campione

Iva Carruthers

Doug Fuchs

Lynn Fuchs

Steve Graham

Karen Harris

Jan Hirshberg

Anne McKeough

Peter Pannell

Michael Pressley

Marsha Roit

Marlene Scardamalia

Marcy Stein

Gerald H. Treadway Jr.

McGraw Hill SRA

Columbus, OH

Acknowledgments

Grateful acknowledgment is given to the following publishers and copyright owners for permissions granted to reprint selections from their publications. All possible care has been taken to trace ownership and secure permission for each selection included. In case of any errors or omissions, the Publisher will be pleased to make suitable acknowledgments in future editions.

I Think I Can

"The Kite" from DAYS WITH FROG AND TOAD by Arnold Lobel. COPYRIGHT © 1979 BY ARNOLD LOBEL. ILLUSTRATIONS COPYRIGHT © 1979 BY ARNOLD LOBEL. Used by permission of HarperCollins Publishers.

THE EASY-TO-READ LITTLE ENGINE THAT COULD by Watty Piper, and illustrated by Mateu. Copyright 1986, 1957, 1930 by Platt & Munk, Publishers. Published by arrangement with Platt & Munk, a division of Grosset & Dunlap, a division of Penguin Young Readers Group, a member of Penguin Group (USA) Inc. THE LITTLE ENGINE THAT COULD, "I THINK I CAN" and all related titles, logos and characters are trademarks of Penguin Group (USA) Inc. PLATT & MUNK and GROSSET & DUNLAP are trademarks of Penguin Group (USA) Inc. All rights reserved. THE LITTLE ENGINE THAT COULD™ is a registered U.S. trademark of Grosset & Dunlap, a division of Penguin Young Readers Group, a member of Penguin Group (USA) Inc.

"Riddles" from IN THE LAND OF WORDS by Eloise Greenfield. Copyright © 2004. Used by permission of HarperCollins.

ITSY, BITSY SPIDER, Text and Illustrations copyright © 1993 by Iza Trapani. Used with permission by Charlesbridge Publishing, Inc. All rights reserved.

WINNERS NEVER QUIT by Mia Hamm, illustrated by Carol Thompson. Copyright © 2004. Used by permission of HarperCollins.

Away We Grow!

HOW A SEED GROWS by Helene J. Jordan, illustrated by Loretta Krupinski. Copyright © 1992 by Helene J. Jordan. Used by permission of HarperCollins Publishers.

"The Garden" from FROG AND TOAD TOGETHER by Arnold Lobel. TEXT COPYRIGHT © 1971, 1972 BY ARNOLD LOBEL. ILLUSTRATIONS COPYRIGHT © 1971, 1972 BY ARNOLD LOBEL. Used by permission of HarperCollins Publishers.

"Saguaro" from CACTUS POEMS, copyright © 1998 by Frank Asch, reprinted by permission of Harcourt, Inc. This material may not be reproduced in any form or by any means without the prior written permission of the publisher. Photographs © Ted Levin.

GREEN AND GROWING by Susan Blackaby, illustrated by Charlene De Lage. Copyright © 2003 by Susan Blackaby. Used with permission from Picture Window Books.

Flowers by Patricia Whitehouse © Harcourt Education Ltd 2006. Harcourt Global Library, part of Harcourt Education Ltd.

"Flowers at Night" From IN THE WOODS, IN THE MEADOW, IN THE SKY by Aileen Fisher. Copyright © 1965 Aileen Fisher. © Renewed 1993 Aileen Fisher. Used by permission of Marian Reiner on behalf of the Boulder Public Library Foundation, Inc.

PLANTS THAT EAT ANIMALS by Allan Fowler. All rights reserved. Reprinted by permission of Children's Press an imprint of Scholarly Library Publishing, Inc.

Photo Credits

ix (cl) © Britstock/Cheryl Hogue; ix (bl) © David Sieren/Visuals Unlimited; viii © Fridmar Damm/zefa/CORBIS; 10–11 © Maurice Faulk/SuperStock; 34 file photo; 76–77 © PhotoDisc/Getty Images, Inc.; 77 (t) Library of Congress, (b) © Klaus Hackenberg/zefa/CORBIS; 94 courtesy of Iza Trapani; 102 (t) © Scala/Art Resource, NY, (b) courtesy of HK Portfolio; 128 (t) © Duomo/CORBIS, (b) courtesy of Carol Thompson; 136–137 © David Muench/CORBIS; 138 © David Aubrey/CORBIS; 139 © Erika Craddock/Photo Researchers, Inc.; 166, 192 file photo; 194–195 © Angelo Cavalli/zefa/CORBIS; 196 © Fridmar Damm/zefa/Corbis; 197 © Ted Levin; 222 (t) courtesy of Susan Blackaby, (b) courtesy of Charlene DeLage; 224–225 © Randy Wells/Getty Images, Inc.; 225 © Leonard Rue Enterprises/Animals Animals/Earth Scenes; 226 © PhotoDisc/Getty Images, Inc.; 227 © Keren Su/CORBIS; 228–229 (bkgd) © Matt Brown/CORBIS; 230 © Nancy Rotenberg; 231 © Dwight R. Kuhn; 232 © Greg Ryan/Sally Beyer; 233 © PhotoDisc/Getty Images, Inc.; 234 © Nancy Rotenberg; 235 © Peter Smithers/CORBIS; 236 © Jay Ireland & Georgienne E. Bradley/Bradleyireland.com; 237 © Michael K. Nichols/National Geographic Image Collection; 238 (inset) © Christopher Knight/Science Photo Library, (bkgd) © Jane Burton/Bruce Coleman, Inc.; 239 (t) © Nancy Rotenberg, (b) © Ed Reschke; 240 © Britstock/Cheryl Hogue; 241 © Joy Spurr/Bruce Coleman, Inc.; 242 © Dwight R. Kuhn; 243 © Rick Wetherbee; 244 © Joe McDonald/McDonald Wildlife Photography; 245 © David Cavagnaro/Visuals Unlimited; 246–247 © Keren Su/CORBIS; 254 © Ed Reschke/Peter Arnold, Inc.; 255 © Patti Murray/Animals Animals; 256–257 © Perennou Nuridsany/Photo Researchers, Inc.; 258 © age fotostock/SuperStock; 259 © David Muench/CORBIS; 260 © Gary Meszaros/Dembinsky Photo Associates; 261 © Gilbert S. Grant/Photo Researchers, Inc.; 262 © Ed Reschke/Peter Arnold, Inc.; 263 © Dan Suzio/Photo Researchers, Inc.; 264 © E. R. Degginger/Dembinsky Photo Associates; 265 © Walter H. Hodge/Peter Arnold, Inc.; 266 © Perennou Nuridsany/Photo Researchers, Inc.; 267 © Claude Nuridsany & Marie Perennou/Photo Researchers, Inc.; 268 © Matt Meadows; 269 © David Sieren/Visuals Unlimited; 270, 271 (b, tl) © Bill Lea/Dembinsky Photo Associates; 271 (tr) © David Sieren/Visuals Unlimited; 272 © Bob Gibbons/FLPA/Photo Researchers, Inc.; 273 © Nuridsany & Perennou/Photo Researchers, Inc.; 274 © Keren Su/Getty Images, Inc.; 275 © Michel Viard/Peter Arnold, Inc.; 276–277 © Walter H. Hodge/Peter Arnold, Inc.; 278–279 © Gunter Marx Photography/CORBIS; 279 © Thomas Mangelsen/Minden Pictures.

SRAonline.com

The McGraw·Hill Companies

Program Authors

Carl Bereiter, Ph.D.
University of Toronto

Andy Biemiller, Ph.D.
University of Toronto

Joe Campione, Ph.D.
University of California, Berkeley

Iva Carruthers, Ph.D.
Northeastern Illinois University

Doug Fuchs, Ph.D.
Vanderbilt University

Lynn Fuchs, Ph.D.
Vanderbilt University

Steve Graham, Ed.D.
Vanderbilt University

Karen Harris, Ed.D.
Vanderbilt University

Jan Hirshberg, Ed.D.
Reading Specialist

Anne McKeough, Ph.D.
University of Toronto

Peter Pannell
Principal, Longfellow Elementary School,
Pasadena, California

Michael Pressley, Ph.D.
Michigan State University

Marsha Roit, Ed.D.
National Reading Consultant

Marlene Scardamalia, Ph.D.
University of Toronto

Marcy Stein, Ph.D.
University of Washington, Tacoma

Gerald H. Treadway, Jr., Ed.D.
San Diego State University

Unit 7 Table of Contents

I Think I Can™

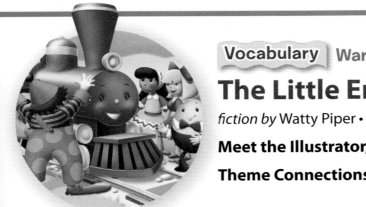

Away We Grow!

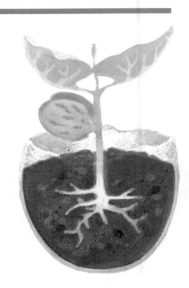

I Think I Can™

Have you ever tried hard to learn something new or to play a new sport? Was it hard to learn to ride a bicycle or to do in-line skating? Did you keep trying until you finally learned? How did it feel?

Fine Art
Theme Connection

Look at *Young Musician* by Maurice Faulk. How do you think it relates to the theme I Think I Can™?

Maurice Faulk. *Young Musician.* 1992.
Acrylic on canvas. 22 x 28 in. Private Collection.

BIG Idea

Why is it important to always try your best?

Read the article to find the meanings of these words, which are also in "The Kite":

✦ meadow
✦ kite

Vocabulary Strategy

Context Clues in the text help you find the meanings of words. Use context clues to find the meaning of *meadow*.

Vocabulary

Warm-Up

I love the meadow. Birds sing as they fly above the grass in the field. Frogs croak from the creek nearby. My grandmother says the meadow is full of laughter. I tell her she is silly. Then she smiles and says, "Perhaps you will try to hear the laughter one day too!"

"Maybe I will," I say.

One day we were flying my kite in the meadow. The wind

stopped. My kite crashed into a bush. There was a loud thud.

"There is no laughter today," I said to my grandmother. Then a squirrel chattered at me. A crow called from above. The wind blew the tall grass. It tickled my legs. I giggled.

"Do you hear laughter in the meadow?" asked my grandmother.

"Yes, I do," I said.

GAME

Guessing Game
Play a guessing game with a partner using the vocabulary words. Ask your partner to guess a vocabulary word after you give a definition. Take turns giving clues.

Concept Vocabulary

The concept word for this lesson is **_disappointed._** _Disappointed_ means "not having a wish or hope come true." Do you think the character in the selection might have felt disappointed when the kite crashed into a bush? Why?

A **fantasy** is a make-believe story that could not happen in the real world.

 Cause and Effect

As you read, look for the causes of the events to help you understand the selection.

Focus Questions

Who discourages Toad from flying a kite? Who helps you when you try to learn something new?

The Kite

written and illustrated by Arnold Lobel

Frog and Toad went out to fly a kite. They went to a large meadow where the wind was strong.

"Our kite will fly up and up," said Frog. "It will fly all the way up to the top of the sky."

"Toad," said Frog, "I will hold the ball of string. You hold the kite and run."

Toad ran across the meadow. He ran as fast as his short legs could carry him.

The kite went up in the air.

It fell to the ground with a bump.

Toad heard laughter.

Three robins were sitting in a bush.

"That kite will not fly," said the robins.

"You may as well give up."

Toad ran back to Frog. "Frog," said
Toad, "this kite will not fly. I give up."

"We must make a second try," said Frog. "Wave the kite over your head. Perhaps that will make it fly."

Toad ran back across the meadow. He
waved the kite over his head. The kite
went up in the air and then fell down
with a thud.

"What a joke!" said the robins. "That kite will never get off the ground."

Toad ran back to Frog. "This kite is a joke," he said. "It will never get off the ground."

"We have to make a third try," said Frog. "Wave the kite over your head and jump up and down. Perhaps that will make it fly."

Toad ran across the meadow again. He waved the kite over his head. He jumped up and down. The kite went up in the air and crashed down into the grass.

"That kite is junk," said the robins.
"Throw it away and go home."

26

Toad ran back to Frog. "This kite is junk," he said. "I think we should throw it away and go home."

"Toad," said Frog, "we need one more try. Wave the kite over your head. Jump up and down and shout UP KITE UP."

Toad ran across the meadow. He waved the kite over his head. He jumped up and down. He shouted, "UP KITE UP!"

The kite flew into the air. It climbed higher and higher.

29

"We did it!" cried Toad.

"Yes," said Frog. "If a running try did not work, and a running and waving try did not work, and a running, waving, and jumping try did not work, I knew that a running, waving, jumping, and shouting try just had to work."

The robins flew out of the bush. But they could not fly as high as the kite.

Frog and Toad sat and watched their kite. It seemed to be flying way up at the top of the sky.

Meet the Author and Illustrator

Arnold Lobel

Arnold Lobel began his career as an illustrator. Then he started to write his own stories. Most of them were about animals, including frogs, toads, grasshoppers, and mice.

I Think I Can

Theme Connections

Within the Selection

1. Why does Toad want to give up?

2. Why does Frog want to keep trying?

Beyond the Selection

3. How do you fly a kite?

4. What kind of weather is helpful when flying kites?

Write about It!

Describe a time you tried something new.

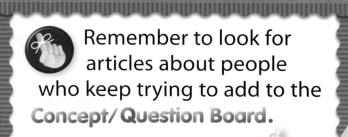

Remember to look for articles about people who keep trying to add to the **Concept/Question Board.**

All about Kites

March is a **windy** month. It is a great month to fly a kite. Kites come in all shapes, sizes, and colors.

Kites are like sailboats in the sky. **Air** pushes them along like beautiful boats. The string on the end of a kite keeps it from blowing away.

Because the kite cannot blow away, it goes up and up. If a kite has a long string, it can go high. It is a good idea not to fly kites near trees. Sometimes **wind** can blow kites into tree branches.

A meadow is a great place to fly a kite. Perhaps you will fly a kite one day!

1. Why is the word *windy* boldfaced?

2. Why is a string attached to the end of a kite?

3. Which days are best for flying a kite?

Try It!

Research classroom, library, or online resources to find information about the history of kites.

Read the article to find the meanings of these words, which are also in "The Little Engine That Could" and "Riddles":

* ✦ riddles
* ✦ fine
* ✦ dining car
* ✦ yards

Vocabulary Strategy

Context Clues help you find the meanings of words. Use context clues to find the meaning of *yards*.

Vocabulary

Warm-Up

Jeff opened his gifts. Jeff got a book of riddles and a train set.

Jeff looked at the picture on the box that held his train set. He saw tracks. He saw lots of train cars. Jeff saw a shiny engine and a caboose. Jeff saw a fine dining car.

"You don't look happy to have a new train set," said Jeff's dad.

"I like my train, but I want it to look real," said Jeff.

"What would make it look real?" asked his dad.

Jeff thought for a minute. "Trains need yards where they can stay," he said. "And a mountain would be nice."

"We can build a yard," said Jeff's dad. "We can prop your tracks so your train can travel up a mountain."

"Let's start building!" said Jeff.

GAME

Illustrate It! Use each of the vocabulary words to write a new sentence. Draw a picture to go with one of your sentences.

Concept Vocabulary

The concept word in this lesson is *try*. To try is to set out to do something. Some children try to keep their rooms clean. What do you try to do?

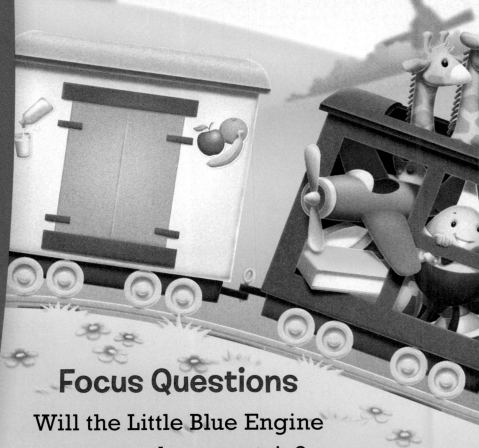

Genre

Fiction is a made-up story that entertains readers.

Comprehension Strategy

☆ **Asking Questions**

As you read, ask yourself questions to help you better understand the selection.

Focus Questions

Will the Little Blue Engine get over the mountain? What did you learn from the Little Blue Engine?

The Little Engine That Could

by Watty Piper

illustrated by Bernard Adnet

Chug chug chug. Puff puff puff.

The little train ran along the tracks.

She was a happy little train. Her cars were full of good things for boys and girls.

There were all kinds of toy animals.

Giraffes with long necks,

teddy bears
with no necks,

and even a
baby elephant.

44

There were all kinds of dolls.

Dolls with blue eyes
and yellow hair,

dolls with brown
eyes and brown hair,

and the funniest toy
clown you ever saw.

There were toy trucks, airplanes, and boats. There were picture books, games, and drums to play.

The little train carried every kind of toy that boys or girls could want.

But that was not all. The little train
carried good things to eat, too.

Big, round oranges . . .

 fat, red apples . . .

long, yellow bananas . . .

 fresh, cold milk . . .

and lollipops to eat
after dinner.

47

The little train was taking all these good things to the other side of the mountain.

"How happy the boys and girls will be to see me!" said the little train. "They will like the toys and good food that I am bringing."

But all at once the train came to a
stop. She did not move at all.

"Oh dear," said the little train.
"What can be the matter?"

She tried to start up again. She tried
and tried. But her wheels just would
not turn.

"We can help," said the toy animals.

The clown and the animals climbed out of their cars. They tried to push the little train.

But she did not move.

"We can help, too," said the dolls.
And they got out and tried to push.

Still the little train did not move.

The toys and dolls did not know what
to do.

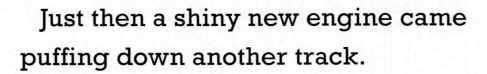

Just then a shiny new engine came puffing down another track.

"Maybe that engine can help us!" cried the clown.

He began to wave a red flag. The Shiny New Engine slowed down.

The dolls and toys called out to him.
"Our engine is not working," they said.
"Please pull our train over the mountain.
If you do not, the boys and girls will not
have any toys or good food."

The Shiny New Engine was not friendly.

"You want *me* to pull *you?*" he asked. "That is not what I do. I carry people. They sit in cars with soft seats. They look out big windows. They eat in a nice dining car. They can even sleep in a fine sleeping car.

"*I* pull the likes of you? I should say not!"

Off went the Shiny New Engine without another word.

How sad all the toys and dolls felt!

Then the toy clown called out, "Here comes another engine. A big, strong one. Maybe *this* engine will help us."

Again the clown waved his flag. The Big Strong Engine came to a stop.

The toys and dolls called out together, "Please help us, Big Strong Engine. Our train is not working. But you can pull us over the mountain.

"You must help us. Or the boys and girls will not have any toys to play with or good food to eat."

But the Big Strong Engine did not want to help.

"I do not pull toys," he said. "I pull cars full of heavy logs. I pull big trucks. I have no time for the likes of you."

And away puffed the Big Strong Engine without another word.

By this time the little train was no longer a happy train.

And the dolls and toys were ready to cry.

But the clown called out, "Look! Look! Another engine is coming. A little blue engine. A very little one. Maybe *this* engine will help us."

The Little Blue Engine was a happy
engine.

She saw the clown waving his red
flag and stopped at once.

"What is the matter?" she asked in a
kind way.

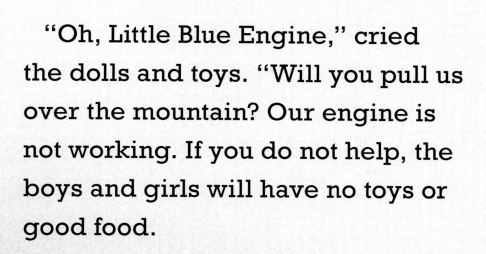

"Oh, Little Blue Engine," cried the dolls and toys. "Will you pull us over the mountain? Our engine is not working. If you do not help, the boys and girls will have no toys or good food.

"Just over the mountain.

"Please, please help us."

"Oh my," said the Little Blue Engine. "I am not very big. And I do not pull trains. I just work in the yards. I have never even been over the mountain."

"But we *must* get there before the children wake up," said the toys and dolls. "Please?"

The Little Blue Engine looked at the dolls and toys. She could see that they were not happy.

She thought about the children on the other side of the mountain. Without toys or good food, they would not be happy either.

The Little Blue Engine pulled up
close. She took hold of the little train.
The toys and dolls climbed back into
their cars.

At last the Little Blue Engine said, "I think I can climb up the mountain. I think I can. I think I can."

Then the Little Blue Engine began to pull. She tugged and she pulled. She pulled and she tugged.

Puff, puff, chug chug went the little engine. "I think I can. I think I can," she said. Slowly, slowly, the train started to move. The dolls and toys began to smile and clap.

Puff puff, chug chug.

Up the mountain went the Little Blue Engine. And all the time she kept saying, "I think I can, I think I can, I think I can. . . ."

Up, up, up. The little engine climbed and climbed.

67

At last she reached the top of the mountain.

Down below lay the city.

"Hurray! Hurray!" cried the dolls and animals.

"The boys and girls will be so happy," said the toy clown. "All because you helped us, Little Blue Engine."

The Little Blue Engine just smiled.

But as she puffed down the mountain, the Little Blue Engine seemed to say . . .

"I thought I could. I thought I could. I thought I could. I thought I could."

Meet the Illustrator

Bernard Adnet

Many of Bernard Adnet's illustrations are in children's books. Animals, Africa, planets, and earthquakes are some of his favorite things to illustrate.

I Think I Can

Theme Connections

Within the Selection

1. How does the Little Blue Engine keep trying?

2. What do we learn about the Little Blue Engine?

Across Selections

3. Think about Frog in "The Kite." How is he similar to the Little Blue Engine?

Beyond the Selection

4. Have you helped someone learn something new?

Write about It!

Describe a time you tried your best. What was the outcome?

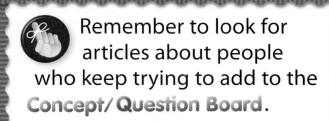

Remember to look for articles about people who keep trying to add to the **Concept/Question Board**.

Genre

Poetry is a special kind of writing in which sounds and meanings of words are combined to create ideas and feelings.

Comprehension Strategy

☆ Clarifying

As you read, check to make sure you understand what you are reading, and then clarify any difficult words or phrases.

Riddles

from *In the Land of Words*
by Eloise Greenfield
illustrated by Fabricio Vanden Broeck

Focus Question

What does it mean to give up?

The ones I like the most
are the ones that make you
think and think,
while everybody waits,
hoping you'll give up.

Give up? Not me.

I'll get it.
You'll see.

75

Science Inquiry

Wheels

Long ago it was hard to travel. People used to walk to get places.

The Early Wheel

One of the best inventions was the wheel. The first wheel was made thousands of years ago. We do not know who made it.

The first wheels were made of wood. They had the shape of a disk. Horses pulled carts that moved over wheels. Travel took a long time.

The Wheel Today

Today we see wheels on cars and trains. We see fine wheels on bicycles. Wheels make getting around fast and easy.

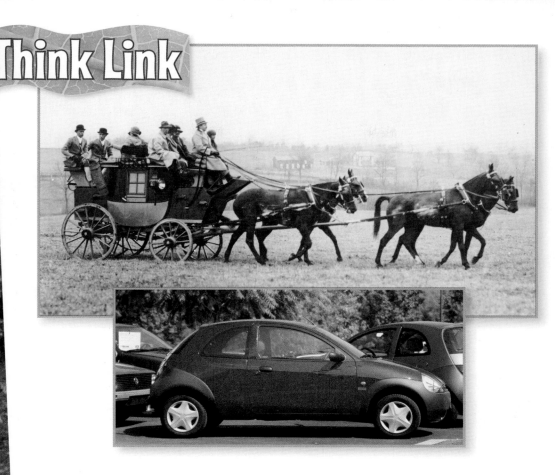

1. How is the heading before the second paragraph helpful?

2. Why do you think travel might have been difficult with early wheels? Make a list of reasons.

3. We know cars, trains, and bicycles have wheels. What other moving things have wheels?

Try It!

Make a list of small, medium, and large wheels.

The Itsy Bitsy Spider
as told and illustrated by Iza Trapani

Focus Questions
Where do spiders spin webs? What does it mean to reach a goal?

Read the article to find the meanings of these words, which are also in "The Itsy Bitsy Spider" and "The Hare and the Tortoise":

✦ **dew**
✦ **pace**
✦ **silky**

Vocabulary Strategy

Context clues in the text help you find the meanings of words. Use context clues to find the meaning of *dew*.

78

Vocabulary

Warm-Up

It was early morning. The dew was still on the field. The spider looked for a place to make her web. "That waterspout looks like a bad place to me," she said. "If it rains, my web will be washed away."

The spider did not give up. The sun warmed the farm and all the animals. "I think I will try to find a home in the barn," said the spider.

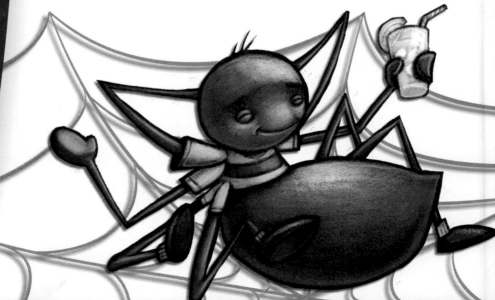

The spider looked into the stalls. "These are too dirty," she said. Then she looked under an old horse cart and smiled to herself.

The spider spun and spun at a fast pace. She wove until she had a silky new home.

GAME

Sentences and Illustrations Game
Make a new sentence for each of the vocabulary words. Have a partner draw a picture to go with at least one sentence.

Concept Vocabulary

The concept word for this lesson is *challenge.* A challenge is something that tests your skill. It can be a challenge to learn new words. Can you think of a game that is a challenge to you?

Genre

Rhyming Fiction uses rhyme to entertain readers.

Comprehension Strategy

⭐ **Visualizing** As you read, picture in your mind what is happening in the selection.

The Itsy Bitsy Spider

as told and illustrated
by Iza Trapani

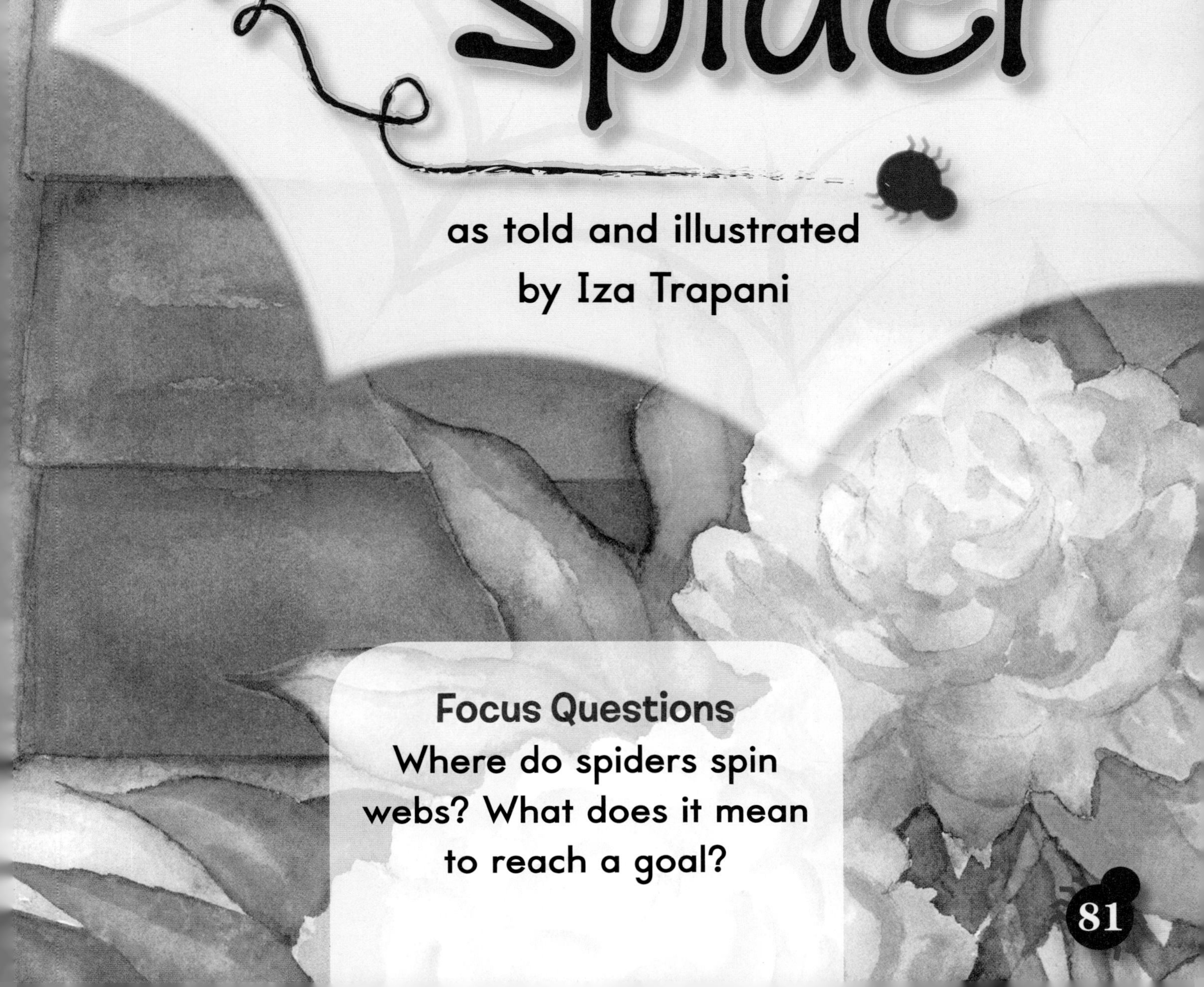

Focus Questions
Where do spiders spin
webs? What does it mean
to reach a goal?

The itsy bitsy spider

Climbed up the waterspout.

Down came the rain

And washed the spider out.

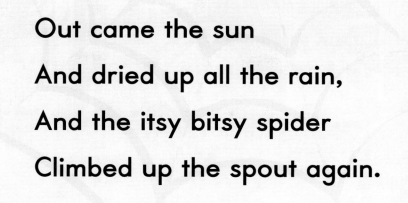

Out came the sun
And dried up all the rain,
And the itsy bitsy spider
Climbed up the spout again.

The itsy bitsy spider

Climbed up the kitchen wall.

Swoosh! went the fan

And made the spider fall.

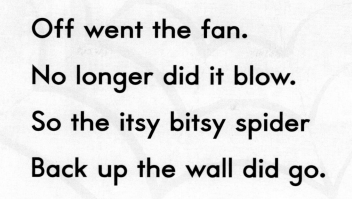

Off went the fan.

No longer did it blow.

So the itsy bitsy spider

Back up the wall did go.

The itsy bitsy spider

Climbed up the yellow pail.

In came a mouse

And flicked her with his tail.

Down fell the spider.

The mouse ran out the door.

Then the itsy bitsy spider

Climbed up the pail once more.

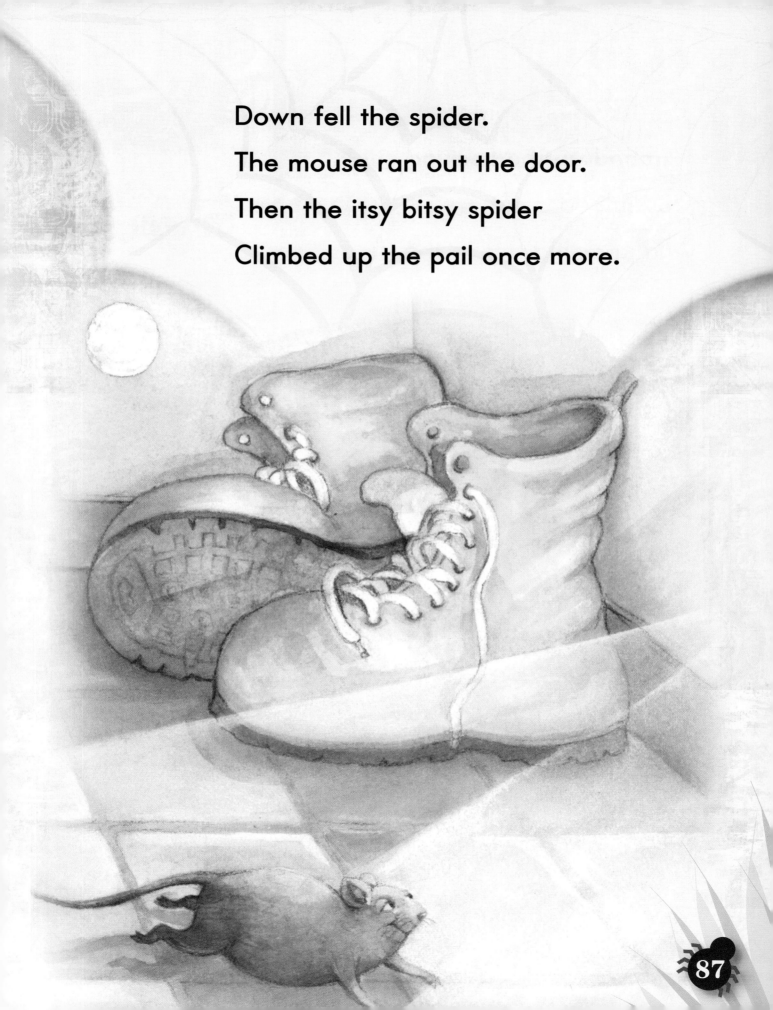

The itsy bitsy spider
Climbed up the rocking chair.
Up jumped a cat
And knocked her in the air.

Down plopped the cat
And when he was asleep,
The itsy bitsy spider
Back up the chair did creep.

The itsy bitsy spider
Climbed up the maple tree.
She slipped on some dew
And landed next to me.

Out came the sun
And when the tree was dry,
The itsy bitsy spider
Gave it one more try.

91

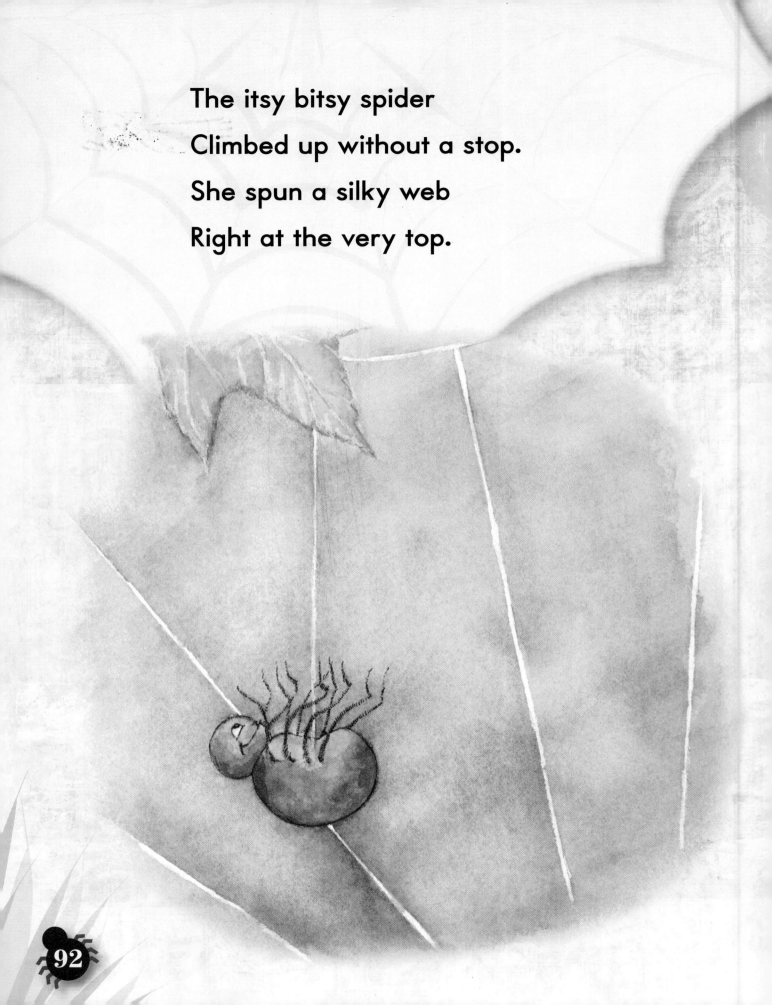

The itsy bitsy spider
Climbed up without a stop.
She spun a silky web
Right at the very top.

She wove and she spun

And when her web was done,

The itsy bitsy spider

Rested in the sun.

93

Iza Trapani

Iza Trapani was born in Poland. Now she lives in New York. She has written and illustrated many children's books. Many of the books Trapani has illustrated include animals because she likes them so much. She also enjoys being in the mountains, where she likes to climb, bicycle, and ski.

Theme Connections

Within the Selection

1. When things get in her way, what does the spider do?

2. Why does the spider keep trying to climb?

Across Selections

3. How is "The Itsy Bitsy Spider" like "The Little Engine That Could"?

Beyond the Selection

4. The spider works very hard. How does it feel to finally reach a goal?

Remember to look for articles about people or animals who keep trying to add to the **Concept/ Question Board.**

*by **Aesop***

*retold by **Nigel St. John IV***

*illustrated by **David Austin Clar***

Focus Questions

Does the fastest runner always win every race? Can you be successful if you work slowly?

The Tortoise and the Hare

The hare always talked
about his speed. "I'm quicker
than the wind. No one could beat
me in a race," he would say. He even
teased the tortoise. "You must be
the slowest animal in the world."

"Is that right?" replied the tortoise.
"I'll race you. And I will win."

"Ha!" replied the hare. "You make me laugh! Let's race and see."

On the day of the race, all the animals met to see the tortoise race the hare. The fox agreed to be the judge of the race. Finally, the fox yelled "Go!"

99

The hare ran so far ahead of the tortoise that he decided to take a nap. Meanwhile, the tortoise kept moving forward. He kept a steady pace. On and on he went down the path. He passed the sleeping hare.

Finally he reached the finish line. Just then the hare woke up and saw the tortoise. With a mad dash he raced toward the finish line. It was too late. The tortoise had already won.

Meet the Author

Aesop

More than two thousand years ago, a man named Aesop liked to tell stories. Aesop traveled a lot, telling wise and entertaining fables. A fable is a very short story that teaches a lesson. Aesop told many fables using animal characters.

Meet the Illustrator

David Austin Clar

In grade school, David Austin Clar was always chosen to draw on the school board. He used his artistic talent in an advertising and design career. Clar enjoys photography, music, art, history, and cooking.

I Think I Can

Theme Connections

Within the Selection

1. Which animal tries harder to win?

2. What will happen if the hare tries harder during the race?

Across Selections

3. How is "The Tortoise and the Hare" like "The Itsy Bitsy Spider"?

4. How are the two stories different?

Beyond the Selection

5. What does it take to win a game or race?

6. Why is it important to give your best effort?

Remember to look for articles about people competing in races to add to the **Concept/Question Board**.

Wintertime

Winter Weather

Many people like winter. Sometimes it snows in the winter.

Some people like to sled down snowy hills at a steady pace. Other people like to take winter walks.

Winter Fun

Many people roll silky snow into balls to make snowmen or snow forts. Other people like to stay inside.

Out Comes the Sun

When the sun comes out, it warms the air. When it is above freezing, the snow begins to melt. Snowmen and snow forts turn to puddles.

1. How is the heading for the last paragraph helpful?

2. Why might a snowman melt?

3. Do you think snow is more fun than rain? Explain.

Try It!

Make a list of things you can do in the snow.

Read the article to find the meanings of these words, which are also in "Winners Never Quit":

✦ stomped
✦ rather

Vocabulary Strategy

Word Structure gives us clues about a word's meaning. Look at the word *stomped*. Use the meaning of the suffix *-ed* to determine the meaning of the word.

Vocabulary

Warm-Up

Juan stomped his foot. "May I play now?" he pleaded.

"I want everyone to have a chance to play," said Coach Lee. "You played the first half."

Juan nodded. "I know," he said, "but I would rather play than sit on the bench."

Coach Lee grinned. "We work as a team," he said. "The other players need you to cheer for them."

The boys dribbled down the court at a steady pace. The ball almost went out of bounds, but it was saved by the other team.

The ball sailed near the net. A tall boy on the other team blocked the shot. Juan's team lost.

After the game Coach Lee gave his team a pep talk. He said, "We succeed every time we play a game because we work together and try our hardest."

Guessing Game
Choose a partner, and play a guessing game using the vocabulary words. Ask your partner which word means "to walk heavily; to stamp with one foot." If your partner correctly guesses *stomped,* he or she can choose the next vocabulary word.

Concept Vocabulary

The concept word for this lesson is ***success.*** Success is what you hope for. Sometimes success comes in winning a game. Other times success comes in learning how to play the game. Think about a time you had success at school.

Genre

Realistic Fiction is a make-believe story that could happen in real life.

Winners

Comprehension Strategy

☆ **Making Connections**

As you read, make connections between what you know and what you are reading.

Focus Questions

Why is it okay for Mia to lose? Why is it important to work as a team?

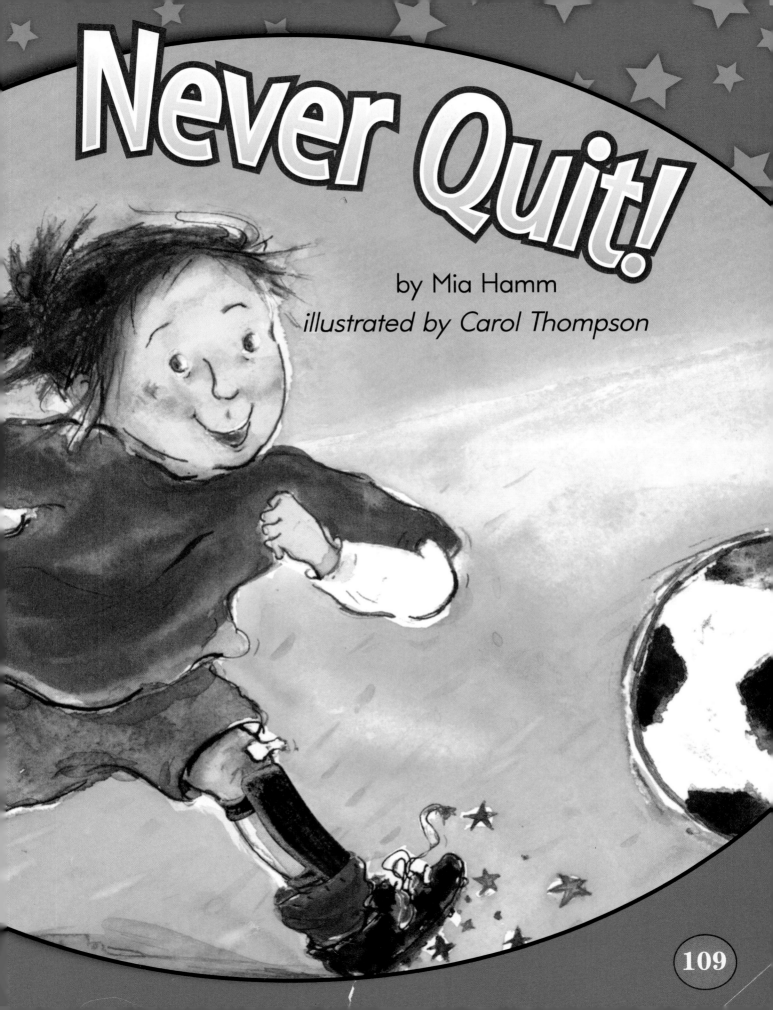

Never Quit!

by Mia Hamm

illustrated by Carol Thompson

Mia loved basketball.
Mia loved baseball.

But most of all, Mia
loved soccer. She played
every day with her
brothers and sisters.

Tap, tap, tap. Her toes kept the ball right where she wanted it. Then, *smack!* She'd kick the ball straight into the net. Goal! Everybody on her team would cheer.

But sometimes it didn't work that way.

One day, no matter how hard she tried, Mia couldn't score a goal.

The ball sailed to the left of the net.

Or to the right.

Or her sister Lovdy, the goalie, saved the ball with her hands.

No goal.
No cheering.

"Too bad, Mia," her brother Garrett said. "Better luck next time!"

But Mia didn't want better luck next time. She wanted better luck *now*.

"I Quit!"

Mia said.

"You can't quit!" Lovdy said.
"Then we'll only have two
people on our team."

"Come on, Mia," her sister Caroline pleaded. "You always quit when you start losing."

"Just keep playing, Mia," Garrett said. "It'll be fun."

But losing wasn't fun. Mia stomped back to the house.

"Quitter!" Lovdy yelled. Mia didn't care. She'd rather quit than lose.

The next day, Mia ran outside, ready to play soccer. When she got there, the game had already started.

"Hey!" she yelled. "Why didn't you wait for me?"

Garrett stopped playing.

"Sorry, Mia," he said. "But quitters can't play on my team."

"Yeah," said Lovdy. "If you can't learn to lose, you can't play."

Garrett passed the ball to Tiffany. Martin ran to steal it. Tiffany dashed around him and took a shot at the goal. Lovdy blocked it.

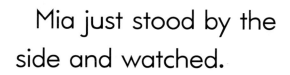
Mia just stood by the side and watched.

The next day, Garrett picked Mia
first for his team.

Mia got the ball. She dribbled down
the field. *Smack!* She kicked the ball
toward the goal.

And Lovdy caught it. **No goal.**
No cheering.

"Too bad, Mia," Garrett said. "Better luck next time."

Mia felt tears in her eyes.

"She's going to quit," whispered Lovdy. "I *knew* it."

Mia still hated losing. But she didn't hate losing as much as she loved soccer.

"Ready to play?" asked Garrett. Mia nodded.

Garrett grinned at her. He passed her the ball.

Mia ran down the field. **Tap, tap, tap** with her toes. The ball stayed right with her, like a friend. She got ready to kick it into the goal.

Mia kicked the ball as hard as she could.

Maybe she'd score the goal. Maybe she wouldn't.

But she was playing.

And that was more important than winning or losing . . .

. . . because **winners** never quit!

Meet the Author

Mia Hamm

Mia Hamm is one of the best women's soccer players in the world. She helped the U.S. Women's Soccer team win a gold medal at the 1996 and 2004 Olympics.

Meet the Illustrator

Carol Thompson

Carol Thompson has created artwork for more than forty children's books. Many of her illustrations have won awards.

I Think I Can

Theme Connections

Within the Selection

1. Why does Mia want to quit?

2. What lesson does Mia learn from her friends?

Across Selections

3. How is "Winners Never Quit!" like "The Tortoise and the Hare"?

4. How are the two stories different?

Beyond the Selection

5. What does it mean to be a team player?

Write about It!

Describe a time you played on a team.

Remember to look for pictures of people who try their best in sports to add to the **Concept/ Question Board.**

The Way to Succeed

I want to be the best pitcher at school. My grandpa told me the way to succeed is to watch winners. He said winners don't always win, but they try their best. My sister Jen is a winner.

Jen is the best skater I know. She practices all the time. Jen can spin and jump. She can glide across the ice gracefully. Sometimes Jen falls. Sometimes Jen loses.

Whenever she loses, she shakes the other skater's hand. Losing makes Jen practice even harder.

Grandpa says Jen is successful. He says she's a winner all the time. Jen would rather do her best than win.

1. Which word in the first sentence lets you know that this selection is a narrative?

2. Do you think a team that loses can win in other ways?

3. How do you feel when you lose?

Try It!

Make a list of ways to be a good sport. Share your ideas with others.

Test Prep

Test-Taking Strategy: Listening Carefully

When you take a test, listen carefully. You will have to answer different kinds of questions on a test. Listening carefully will help you choose the correct answers.

Listening Carefully

Listen to the sound and identify the spelling that makes that sound. The sound is /b/. Which spelling makes the /b/ sound?

○ m   ○ b   ○ s

The middle spelling is the letter *b*. Point to the circle next to the letter *b*. The spelling *b* makes the /b/ sound.

Here is another question. Listen carefully to the question. Then listen to the choices to figure out the correct answer.

The letters below are *m, m,* and *s.* Two of the letters are the same. One is different. Which letter is different?

○ m   ○ m   ○ s

The third one is different. Point to the circle next to the third letter. It is an *s,* and the other letters are *m*'s.

Even though these two questions look alike, you had to listen carefully to choose the correct answer. Whenever you take a test, be sure to listen carefully.

STOP

Test-Taking Practice

Read the story below. Then complete the test on the next page.

Test Tip

Listen carefully to your teacher.

Dan Tried Again

Dan was a speed skater. He liked to race. Everyone thought he would win a medal in 1988. He did not.

In 1992, Dan tried again. He was ready for the race. He fell on the ice. Dan did not win.

For two years, Dan worked hard. Then he tried again. When the race started, he skated fast. Dan won the race! Everybody was happy. Dan was happy!

Complete the test below.

Test Tip

Read each question carefully.

1. What was Dan's sport?

○ skiing

○ swimming

○ speed skating

2. What happened in 1992?

○ Dan was tired.

○ Dan fell.

○ Dan got sick.

3. How many times in the story did Dan try to win?

○ one time

○ two times

○ three times

STOP

Away We Grow!

Plants grow in many places around the world. What kinds of plants have you seen? Where did you see them? What did they look like?

Fine Art Theme Connection

Look at the photo *Flowering Cacti in California Desert* by David Muench. How many different plants do you see?

David Muench. *Flowering Cacti in California Desert.* 1981–1982.
Anza-Borrego Desert State Park, California.

BIG
Idea

What do plants
need to grow?

137

Read the article to find the meanings of these words, which also appear in "How a Seed Grows":

✦ aside

✦ root

Vocabulary Strategy

Context Clues in the text help you find the meanings of words. Use context clues to find the meanings of *aside* and *root*.

Vocabulary

Warm-Up

Jacob looked at the packages of flower seeds. "I like the pale colors best," he told his father.

"Set aside a package of the pink ones for later," his father said.

Jacob couldn't wait to plant the seeds. He would start them in cups. "You will have to water them," said Jacob's father.

"I know the rain soaks them outside. Should I use that much water?" Jacob asked his father.

"You don't need that much," he said. "But you'll need enough water to reach each root at the bottom of the cup."

Jacob put the cups in a sunny window. He watered his seeds. He watched them grow.

Jacob put his plants in the garden. "I'll have the best flowers on our street," he told his father.

Story Use each of the selection vocabulary words to write a story about a garden. Draw a picture to go with your story.

Concept Vocabulary

The concept word for this lesson is *garden.* A garden is a place flowers and vegetables grow. Do you have a garden in your yard? What kinds of flowers or vegetables do you grow in your garden?

Genre

Realistic Fiction is a make-believe story that could happen in the real world.

Comprehension Strategy

 **Asking Questions**

As you read, ask yourself questions to help you better understand the selection.

How a SEED

Focus Question

How does a seed grow?

GROWS

by Helene J. Jordan

illustrated by Loretta Krupinski

A seed is a little plant. It is a plant
that has not started to grow.

Apple trees and daisies, carrots and corn, clover and wheat, all grow from seeds.

Here is a tree seed.

Someday it will be a tree like this.

144

Here is a flower seed.

Someday it will be a flower like this.

Some seeds grow slowly. These are the seeds of an oak tree.

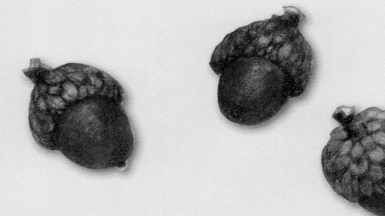

An oak tree grows very, very slowly. Suppose you planted an oak tree seed. You would be a father or a mother, or even a grandfather or a grandmother, and the oak tree would still be growing.

Some seeds grow fast.
This is a bean seed.

It grows very fast. It grows so fast
that it becomes a bean plant in just
a few weeks.

You can plant bean seeds yourself.
We used pole beans. You can use pole
beans, bush beans, or lima beans.

You can plant the seeds in eggshells
or tin cans or old cups or little
flowerpots. Be sure that your containers
have holes in the bottom.

We used eggshells. We used a pencil to make holes in the eggshells.

We filled twelve eggshells with soil like this.

We made a hole in the soil with a finger, like this.

When you have made
a hole in the soil,
plant a bean seed in it.
Plant one seed in
each hole.

Cover the seed with soil.

Sprinkle the soil carefully with a little water.

Number the shells. Write the number 1 on the first shell. Put the number 2 on the next shell. Keep going until all of the shells are numbered from 1 to 12.

Put all the eggshells in an egg carton.

Put the carton in sunlight on a windowsill.

Some bean seeds grow faster than others. Our seeds began to grow in three days. Your bean seeds may take a little longer.

You won't be able to see your seeds growing yet. They start to grow under the soil where you can't see them.

Water your seeds a little every day.

The water soaks into the seeds. The seeds begin to grow.

More water soaks into the seeds. The seeds get fatter and fatter.

Wait for three days and then dig up seed Number 1.

It may be soft. It may be fat. Maybe it will look the same as it did before.

Soon the seed will grow so fat that its skin will pop off.

In two more days dig up seed Number 2.

155

Maybe it will look different now. Maybe
the skin of this seed will be loose.

Now a root starts to grow. The root grows from one side of the bean seed.

The root pushes down into the soil, down and down.

Dig up seed Number 3. Can you see the root? Does it look like this?

If you do not see a root, wait for another day. Then dig up seed Number 4.

After a few more days, dig up seed Number 5. Something else is happening. Little roots will be growing from the big root. They look like tiny white hairs. They are called root hairs.

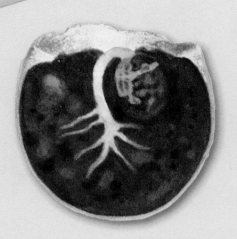

Day after day the roots and root
hairs push down into the soil.

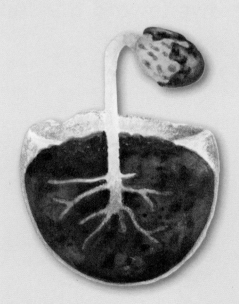

Day after day the bean seeds are
pushed up. The soil is pushed aside.

Watch your seeds. Soon you will see pale shoots push through the soil. A shoot is the beginning of a green plant. A shoot grows toward the sun.

Watch your seeds. Some may have come through the ground. Some may have broken open. Maybe some of your seeds have not started to grow.

How many are growing? Count them.

The bean seeds grow fast.
The shoots turn green.

The leaves come next. Now your
bean seeds are bean plants. They
look like this.

How many of your bean seeds are bean plants?

A seed needs many things to grow.

It needs soil

and water

and sun.

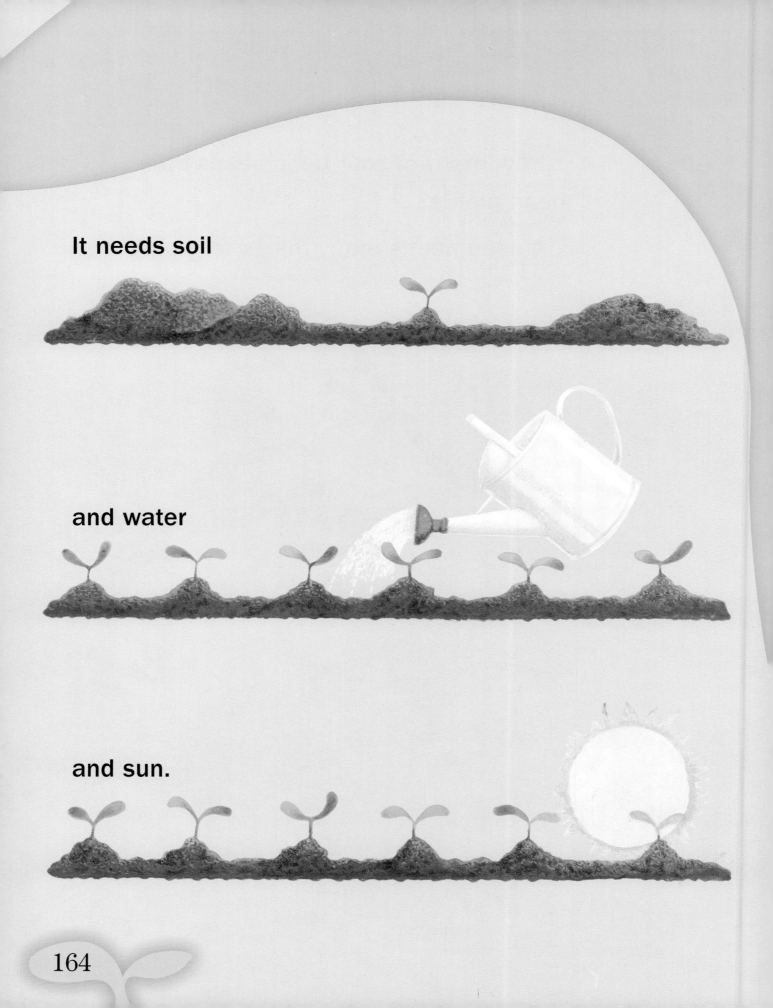

If a seed has all these things, it will grow into a plant. It will grow into the same kind of plant that it came from— an apple tree, or a daisy, or carrots, or corn. It will grow into clover or it will grow into a bean plant like the ones you planted.

Meet the Author

Helene J. Jordan

In school Helene J. Jordan's favorite subject was science! She used what she learned in school to later write about science in magazines for grown-ups. Jordan wrote books for children to include them in the fun of learning about science.

Meet the Illustrator

Loretta Krupinski

Working in a garden is fun for Loretta Krupinski. She grew all the bean plants she drew in *How a Seed Grows*. She lives in Connecticut with her daughter and her cat.

Away We Grow!

Theme Connections

Within the Selection

1. How does a seed become a plant?

2. What kinds of plants grow from seeds?

Beyond the Selection

3. How is the growth of a plant like the growth of a person?

4. Do all plants grow at the same speed?

Write about It!

Describe a plant that is in your house or neighborhood.

Remember to look for articles about plants to add to the **Concept/Question Board**.

Science Inquiry

How Seeds Grow

Plants need sun and water. Ms. Green's class did an experiment to show why plants need sun and water. They used three clear cups, seeds, soil, water, and sun.

They filled each cup with soil. They labeled the cups A, B, and C. They put one seed into the soil in each cup.

They put Cup A in a sunny area. They watered the seed each day.

They put Cup B aside where there was no sun. They watered the seed each day.

They put Cup C in the sun. They did not give it any water.

1. Look at the diagram. Which plant grew the most?

2. Why did Ms. Green's class do an experiment?

3. Look at the diagram. Write a sentence about the plants.

Try It!

With an adult's help, try this experiment at home.

Genre
A fantasy is a make-believe story that could not happen in the real world.

Comprehension Skill
☆ Drawing
Conclusions
As you read, use what you learn about the characters and events to help you better understand the selection.

The
Garden
written and illustrated by
Arnold Lobel

Focus Question
How long does it take for a seed to grow?

172   173

Read the article to find the meanings of these words, which are also in "The Garden" and "Saguaro":

✦ flower
✦ tight
✦ quite
✦ shouted

Vocabulary Strategy

Context Clues in the text help you find the meanings of words. Use context clues to find the meaning of *quite.*

Vocabulary

Warm-Up

My mom and I read a book of poems about plants. We read about carrots, corn, and beans. We agreed it would be fun to plant our own garden.

We went to the store to buy vegetable and flower seeds.

Next, we pulled weeds. The weeds were slippery. I had to get a tight grip on the plants. It took quite a long time! After that, we dug into the dirt. While digging, I heard a bee buzzing. It frightened me! I shouted for mom.

"It's okay," she said. "Bees are a part of every garden. They help flowers grow."

We spent the day in the hot sun. I was tired but excited for our garden. I can't wait to eat the vegetables and pick the pretty flowers.

GAME

Story Write a new sentence using each of the selection vocabulary words. Can your sentences make a new story?

Concept Vocabulary

The concept word for this lesson is ***patient.*** To be patient is to be able to wait quietly for something you want. Talk about why it is important for people to be patient. What can happen when people are not patient?

The Garden

written and illustrated by
Arnold Lobel

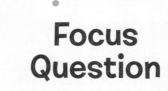

Frog was in his garden. Toad came walking by. "What a fine garden you have, Frog," he said.

"Yes," said Frog. "It is very nice, but it was hard work."

"I wish I had a garden," said Toad.

"Here are some flower seeds. Plant them in the ground," said Frog, "and soon you will have a garden."

"How soon?" asked Toad.

"Quite soon," said Frog.

Toad ran home. He planted the flower seeds. "Now seeds," said Toad, "start growing."

Toad walked up and down a few times. The seeds did not start to grow. Toad put his head close to the ground and said loudly, "Now seeds, start growing!"

Toad looked at the ground again.
The seeds did not start to grow. Toad
put his head very close to the ground
and shouted, "NOW SEEDS, START
GROWING!"

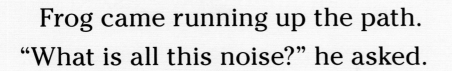

Frog came running up the path. "What is all this noise?" he asked.

"My seeds will not grow," said Toad.

"You are shouting too much," said Frog. "These poor seeds are afraid to grow."

"My seeds are afraid to grow?" asked Toad.

"Of course," said Frog. "Leave them alone for a few days. Let the sun shine on them, let the rain fall on them. Soon your seeds will start to grow."

That night Toad looked out of his window. "Drat!" said Toad. "My seeds have not started to grow. They must be afraid of the dark."

Toad went out to his garden with some candles. "I will read the seeds a story," said Toad. "Then they will not be afraid."

Toad read a long story to his seeds.

All the next day Toad sang songs to
his seeds.

And all the next day Toad read
poems to his seeds.

And all the next day Toad played
music for his seeds.

Toad looked at the ground. The seeds still did not start to grow.

"What shall I do?" cried Toad. "These must be the most frightened seeds in the whole world!"

Then Toad felt very tired, and he fell asleep.

"Toad, Toad, wake up," said Frog. "Look at your garden!"

Toad looked at his garden. Little green plants were coming up out of the ground.

"At last," shouted Toad, "my
seeds have stopped being afraid
to grow!"

"And now you will have a nice garden too," said Frog.

"Yes," said Toad, "but you were right,
Frog. It was very hard work."

Meet the Author and Illustrator

Arnold Lobel

As a child, Arnold Lobel was a daydreamer. He wrote stories and drew pictures for his classmates. He loved to hear Mother Goose stories. When he grew up, Lobel illustrated his favorite Mother Goose rhymes.

Away We Grow!

Theme Connections

Within the Selection

1. Why do Toad's seeds not grow into plants right away?

2. Does Toad's hard work help the seeds grow? Why or why not?

Across Selections

3. Compare how long it took Toad's seeds to grow to the growing time in "Cactus Hotel" and "How a Seed Grows."

Beyond the Selection

4. Have you ever planted anything? What did you do to help it grow?

Remember to post questions about plants in gardens on the **Concept/ Question Board**.

Genre

Poetry is a special kind of writing in which the sounds and meanings of the words are combined to create ideas and feelings.

Comprehension Strategy

☆ Visualizing

As you read, picture in your mind what is happening in the selection.

Saguaro

by Frank Asch

Stand
still.
Grow
slow.
Lift
high
your arms to the sun.
Stand
still.
Grow
slow.
Lift
high
your
flowers to the sky.
Stand
still.
Grow
slow.
Hold
tight
your
water
inside.
Stand
still.
Grow
slow
and let your roots spread wide
and let your roots spread wide.

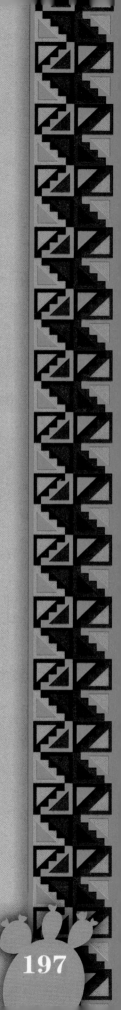

Science Inquiry

The Gazette

First-Grade Class Grows Beans!

by Miguel Muñoz

The first graders have a garden. Students made the garden inside! In winter they planted seeds in cups. They were patient. They waited for the seeds to grow.

In spring, students planted the beans outside. They measured the rainfall. They counted the sunny days. They measured the plants each week. They even kept a chart of how much the plants grew.

Students will enter the beans in the fair. They are quite sure they will win a blue ribbon!

Think Link

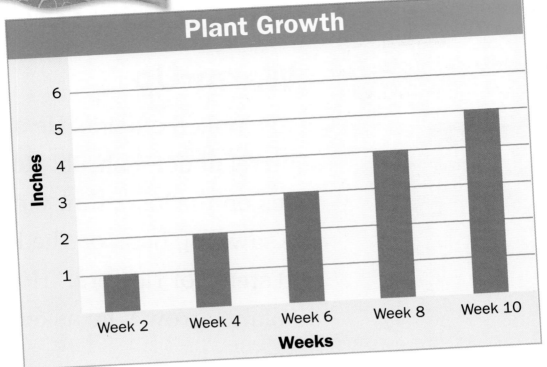

Plant Growth

Inches

6
5
4
3
2
1

Week 2   Week 4   Week 6   Week 8   Week 10

Weeks

1. How is a chart helpful?

2. How do you know that the first graders are patient?

3. Look at the bar graph. How tall were the flowers during Week 8?

Try It!

With the help of an adult, try charting the growth of a plant at home.

Read the article to find the meanings of these words, which are also in "Green and Growing":
+ shrub
+ vine
+ stems
+ energy

Vocabulary Strategy

Context Clues in the text help you find the meanings of words. Use context clues to find the meanings of *vine* and *stems*.

Vocabulary

Warm-Up

Joe looked outside. He saw a squirrel under a shrub. He saw roses on the long, thin vine. Joe saw tiny bugs on the leaves and stems of flowers. "How do plants grow?" he asked his mom.

"Plants need water, air, and soil. They depend on the sun

to grow. The energy from all this helps them grow."

"How do plants get water?" he asked.

"Plants store water in their roots. Most roots grow underground," said Joe's mom. "Let's go outside and take a closer look. We can use our senses to learn more about plants."

Joe and his mom took a deep breath. They walked around the yard and enjoyed the pretty flowers.

GAME

Memory Game Write each vocabulary word on an index card. Then write each word's meaning on another card. Turn over and spread out the cards. Take turns with a partner, trying to match each word with its meaning.

Concept Vocabulary

The concept word for this lesson is *oxygen.* Oxygen is part of the air. All living things need oxygen to live. Plants give off oxygen. Why is oxygen important?

Informational Writing informs or explains something real.

 **Classify and Categorize** As you read, group things and ideas that are alike.

Green and Growing

A Book about Plants

by Susan Blackaby

illustrated by Charlene DeLage

Focus Question

How do you use plants?

All Kinds of Plants

How is a maple tree like a daffodil?

How is a blade of grass like a rosebush?

All of these are living things.

All of these are living things called plants.

A plant can be a tree or a shrub.

A plant can be a flower or a trailing vine.

No matter what they look like or where they live, all green, growing things are alike in some ways.

How Plants Are Alike

Green plants make their own food to grow healthy and strong.

They use their roots to soak up water.

They use their green parts
to soak up air and sunlight.

They use the air, water,
and sunlight to make the
food they need.

Plants cannot move from place to place
the way animals do.

Their roots keep them rooted to one spot.

Animals, wind, and water carry plant
seeds to new places where they can grow.

Plants do not have senses, but they react to light.

They grow up toward the sunlight.

They grow around things that get in their way.

Daisy Means Day's Eye

The daisy's flower opens in the morning. The flower head turns as it follows the sun across the sky. It closes at sunset.

How Plants Are Different

Many plants, like poppies and peach trees, have roots, stems, and leaves.

They have flowers and seeds, too. The seeds can be inside of pods or fruit.

Some plants, like firs and pines and cedars, have needles instead of leaves.

They have seed cones instead of fruit.

Some plants, like grasses, do not have real stems.

Plants can come in all sizes, shapes, and colors.

The smallest plant on Earth is duckweed.

Duckweed is not much bigger than the period at the end of this sentence.

The biggest plant on Earth is the giant redwood.

A very old redwood can be as tall as a 20-story skyscraper.

Plants can grow every which way.
Some plants creep along the ground.

Some plants grow tall and straight.
Some plants climb walls or cliffs.

Plants can grow almost anywhere.

Cactus plants find and store water
in the hot, dry desert.

Pine trees grow tall on windy, snowy
mountain slopes.

Cattails and reeds like boggy, soggy ground.

Lily of the valley grows best in cool, dark places.

How You Use Plants

Think about how you use plants every day. Plants give off oxygen when they make their food. You breathe the oxygen in the air.

You eat plant parts.

Your body uses the energy that was stored in the plants.

What Plant Parts Do You Eat?

Roots: Carrots, Radishes

Stems: Rhubarb, Potato

Leaves: Lettuce, Spinach

Fruits: Bananas, Oranges, Tomatoes, Cucumbers

Seeds: Rice, Corn, Peanuts

Flowers: Brussels Sprouts, Broccoli, Cauliflower

It takes lots of plants to make one bag lunch.

Your shirt, pants, socks, and sneakers came from a cotton plant.

The tree used to make the table grew from a seed no bigger than your thumb.

Parts of a tree were even used to make the bag!

People depend on a world of sprouting seeds, blooming bushes, and towering trees. Think of all the amazing plants that grow in our garden called Earth!

Meet the Author

Susan Blackaby

Writing is not new to Susan Blackaby. She began her career writing textbooks. She is currently writing stories for children. Blackaby lives in Oregon and enjoys spending time with her family.

Meet the Illustrator

Charlene DeLage

Animals and art are passions for Charlene DeLage. In school, she loved to draw her favorite animals. Now she combines her favorite things by drawing pictures for books.

Theme Connections

Within the Selection

1. How are all plants alike?

2. How are some plants different from each other?

Across Selections

3. What did you learn about plants from this selection that you did not learn from the other selections in this unit?

Beyond the Selection

4. What other ways do people use plants?

Write about It!

Describe a time you used a plant.

Remember to look for pictures of different plants to add to the **Concept/ Question Board**.

Cacti and Pine Trees

Cacti

A cactus plant can grow to be almost fifty feet high. Its branches look like huge fingers. Most cacti do not have leaves. They are covered with spines. The spines protect the cactus from animals. Cacti grow in the desert. They do not need much water. Cacti store water in their roots and stems.

Pine Trees

Pine trees do not have leaves either. They have green needles. Pine trees like cool weather. They stay green all year. Pinecones grow on pine trees. At first they are green. Then they are brown and woodlike. Animals use pine trees for shelter.

Think Link

1. How do you know what the second paragraph will be about?

2. How are a cactus and a pine tree the same? How are they different?

3. A cactus does not make a good home for some animals. Explain why.

Try It!

Divide a paper in half. On one side draw a desert picture with lots of cacti. On the other side draw a forest picture with lots of pine trees!

Genre
A photo essay uses photographs and words to inform or explain.

Comprehension Skill

☆ Compare and Contrast
As you read, compare and contrast ideas, characters, and events.

Flowers
by Patricia Whitehouse

Focus Question
What kinds of flowers are there?

228   229

Read the article to find the meanings of these words, which are also in "Flowers" and "Flowers at Night":

✦ bright
✦ petals

Vocabulary Strategy

Apposition tells the definition of a word. The definition follows the word and is set off by commas. Use apposition to find the meaning of *bright*.

Vocabulary

Warm-Up

Theo, the best gardener in town, sang a song. He counted the buds on the daisies. "One bud. Two buds. Three buds! Music helps my flowers grow," he sang.

"Music doesn't help your garden grow," said Theo's wife. "Insects do!"

Theo looked at the pistil, the tiny stalk, in the middle of a daisy. He saw yellow dust on the stamen. He saw butterflies on the bright, or colorful, petals.

Theo knew butterflies carry the pollen to other plants. This helps flowers grow. Theo loved flowers.

He loved bees too. Bees sipped nectar from his flowers. Then the bees went back to their hives and made honey. Theo loved insects almost as much as he loved his flowers!

Draw It! Draw a picture of Theo's flowers. Use the vocabulary words to label the parts of one of the flowers in your picture.

Concept Vocabulary

The concept word for this lesson is **care.** *Care* means "to watch over someone or something." How does a person care for the flowers in a garden?

Genre

A photo-essay uses photographs and words to inform or explain.

Comprehension Skill

☆ **Compare and Contrast**

As you read, compare and contrast ideas, characters, and events.

228

Flowers

by Patricia Whitehouse

Focus Question
What kinds of flowers are there?

What Are Flowers?

stem

Flowers are a part of some plants. They grow on the ends of branches or stems.

Flowers grow on trees, too. These
are an oak tree's flowers.

Why Do Plants Have Flowers?

pollen

stamen

Flowers make seeds. First, a yellow dust called pollen forms on the stamens.

Next, the pollen drops into the pistil.
Then, seeds start to grow.

pistil

Where Do Flowers Come From?

Flowers come from buds. Sun shines on the bud.

When the bud gets enough sunlight, it opens. Then you can see the flower and its colorful petals.

bud

petals

How Big Are Flowers?

orchid

Flowers are many sizes. This orchid is smaller than a coin.

Some flowers are very big. This one is almost as big as a man.

How Many Flowers Can Plants Have?

Some plants have one flower.
Some have more.

A sunflower looks like one flower, but it's not. Each yellow part is one flower!

What Shapes Are Flowers?

Flowers have many shapes.
But flowers on one plant have
the same shape.

Some flowers are round.

These flowers look like birds.

What Do Flowers Smell Like?

Many flowers smell like perfume.
But these flowers smell like skunks!
They are called skunk cabbage.

How Do People Use Flowers?

People use some flowers for food.
When you eat broccoli, you are
eating flowers.

People use some flowers to make perfume. People give flowers as presents.

How Do Animals Use Flowers?

Birds and bugs use flowers for food. They drink a juice called nectar from the flower.

Some bugs hide inside flowers.
They can hide there because their
color matches the flower.

Meet the Author

Patricia Whitehouse

For more than seventeen years, Patricia Whitehouse studied and taught science. Now she is using her knowledge to write books for children. She has written more than one hundred books! Some of them are about zoo animals, science experiments, and exploring space. If you have lots of questions, reading books written by Whitehouse can help you answer them!

Theme Connections

Within the Selection

1. What kinds of plants or flowers are listed in the selection?

2. What are some ways flowers are different from each other?

Across Selections

3. What does this selection tell about plants that "The Garden" does not?

Beyond the Selection

4. What other kinds of flowering plants do you know?

Write about It!

Describe your favorite flower. Include information about the size and color of the flower.

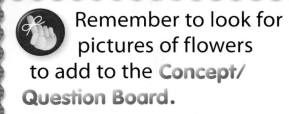

Remember to look for pictures of flowers to add to the Concept/ Question Board.

Poetry is a special kind of writing in which sounds and meanings of words are combined to create ideas and feelings.

Comprehension Strategy

⭐ **Visualizing** As you read, picture in your mind what is happening in the selection.

Focus Question

Why do some flowers open only at night?

FLOWERS AT NIGHT

by Aileen Fisher

illustrated by Maru Jara

Some flowers close their petals,
blue and red and bright,
and go to sleep all tucked away
inside themselves at night.

250

Some flowers leave their petals
like windows open wide
so they can watch the goings-on
of stars and things outside.

Science Inquiry

Living and Nonliving Things

Many living and nonliving things are around us.

Living Things

All plants are living things. All living things need food, air, and water to grow. A flower is a plant. Many petals grow from a flower bud.

Trees are living things. Berries can grow on a bush or vine. Bushes are living things. So are vines.

Nonliving Things

Nonliving things do not need food, air, and water. They do not grow.

We use nonliving things every day. We use ink from pens. Ink and pens are not living things.

1. How did the heading in the second paragraph help you?

2. List something that is living. List something that is nonliving.

3. Flowers are living things. Explain why.

Try It!

Draw something that is living. Write a sentence about it.

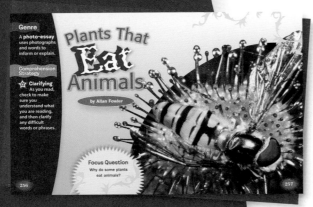

Genre
A photo-essay uses photographs and words to inform or explain.

Comprehension Strategy

⭐ Clarifying As you read, check to make sure you understand what you are reading, and then clarify any difficult words or phrases.

Read the article to find the meanings of these words, which also appear in "Plants That Eat Animals":

✦ **wetlands**
✦ **attracts**
✦ **insects**
✦ **trapping**

Vocabulary Strategy

Context Clues can help you find the meanings of *wetlands* and *trapping*.

Vocabulary

Warm-Up

The ground in wetlands is really wet. It is hard to walk on this land. Walking in wetlands can make you hot and thirsty. You might want to drink a sweet liquid, like fruit juice. You might be so thirsty you want to drink a big

jug, or pitcher, of juice. A sweet drink attracts insects too. Many bugs live in this kind of area. Trapping these bugs between your hands is a bad idea. Some insects have sharp tips that can poke you. These sharp ends can hurt. Be safe in wetlands. Bring a lot to drink. And if someone removes the cover on your drink, put the top back on. Then the bugs won't get to your sweet drink.

GAME

Matching Game Write each vocabulary word on an index card. Then write each word's meaning on its own card. Place the cards facedown, and spread out the cards. Take turns with a partner matching each word with its meaning.

Concept Vocabulary

The concept word for this lesson is **entice.** To entice is to draw in by offering something.

How can you be enticed to eat vegetables?

Plants That Eat Animals

by Allan Fowler

Focus Question

Why do some plants eat animals?

All plants need water and minerals to grow. Most plants get them from the soil.

Some plants grow in soil that has few
minerals in it.

A plant traps
a fly.

They get food by trapping small animals.

The Venus's-flytrap grows in wetlands in North and South Carolina. It is about 12 inches tall and has white flowers.

Venus's-flytrap

Each leaf looks like a clam's shell. It has sharp spines around the edges and soft hairs inside.

The leaf gives off a sweet juice that attracts insects.

A Venus's-flytrap traps a cricket.

When an insect touches the hairs on a Venus's-flytrap leaf, the two halves snap shut.

The plant slowly breaks down the insect's body and removes the minerals.

Then the leaf opens up again.

Sundew plant

Sundew plants grow in wet, boggy
areas all over the world.

Each leaf has soft, red hairs with
drops of sticky liquid on the tips.

When an insect gets stuck to
a few hairs . . .

. . . all the other hairs on that leaf fold
over and hold the insect in place.

After the plant breaks down the insect's body, the hairs open up again.

The sundew is ready for another meal.

Can you guess how the pitcher
plant got its name?

Its leaves are shaped like
a pitcher and hold
a sweet liquid.

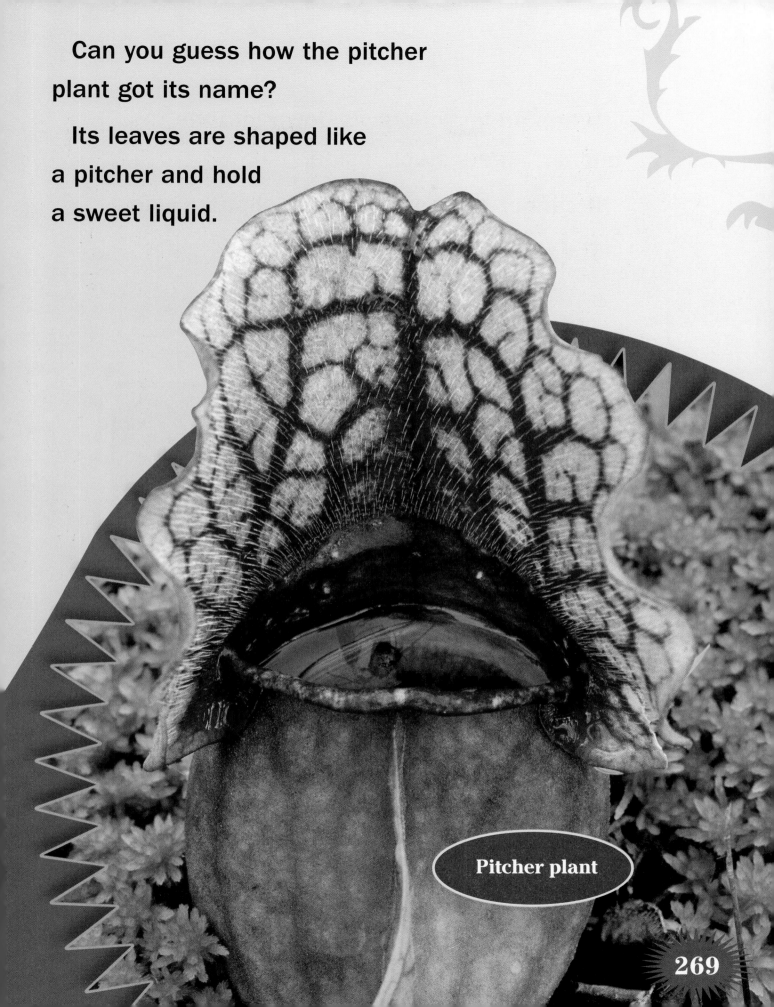

Pitcher plant

When an insect crawls down into the pitcher, it gets stuck inside.

It cannot climb back up the slippery sides.

The insect drowns in the liquid.

There are many different kinds of pitcher plants.

Trumpet pitcher plant

Purple pitcher plant

Flytrap pitcher plant

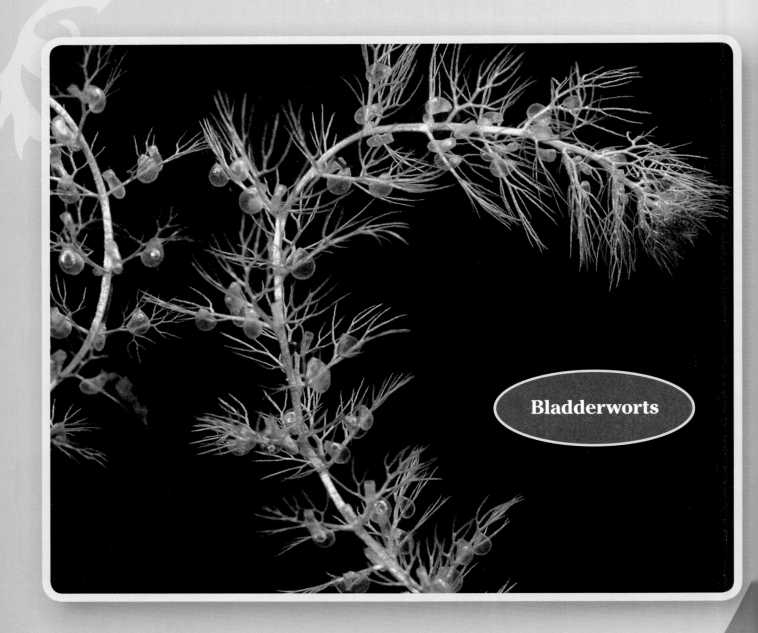

Bladderworts

Bladderworts live in ponds. Their leaves are covered with tiny bags called bladders.

If an insect or small fish touches one of the bladders, it opens up and sucks the animal inside.

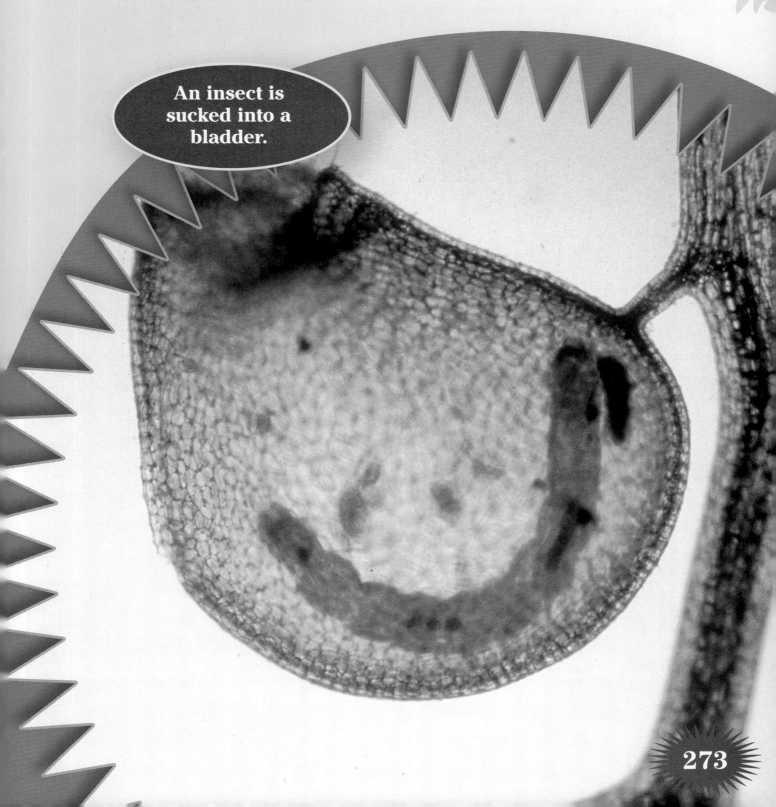

An insect is sucked into a bladder.

You probably know many animals that eat plants.

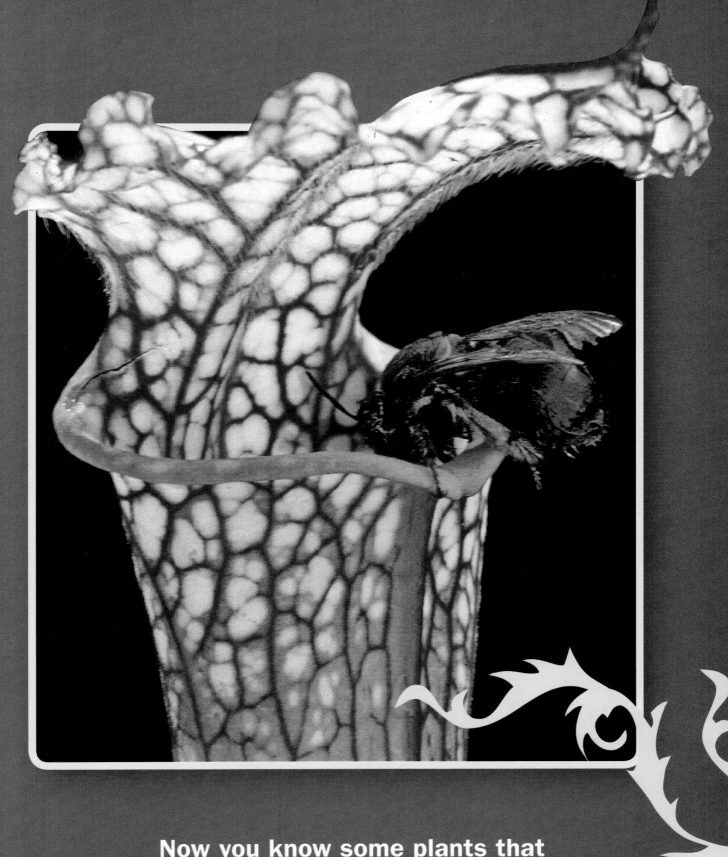

Now you know some plants that
eat animals!

Meet the Author

Allan Fowler

Writing nonfiction books for young readers is Allan Fowler's specialty. He likes to explain how things work and why things happen. Do you know why the moon seems to change shape or how magnets work? You can read books by Fowler to find out. His fact-filled books cover lots of topics, mostly in science. Fowler lives in Chicago and likes to travel when he has the chance.

Away We Grow!

Theme Connections

Within the Selection

1. Why do plants eat animals? What animals do they eat?

2. How do plants trap animals?

Across Selections

3. How are the plants in this selection different from the plants we have read about in other selections?

Beyond the Selection

4. Compare the reasons animals eat plants with the reasons plants eat animals.

Write about It!

Describe the most interesting plant in this selection. Explain why it is interesting.

Remember to look for pictures of plants that eat animals to add to the **Concept/Question Board.**

What Do Birds Eat?

Has anybody ever said, "You eat like a bird"? If they have, you must eat all the time. Birds do!

Fruit and Seeds

Many birds eat fruit and seeds. They may live in trees that grow the fruit or seeds. A bird's home can be like a delicious restaurant!

Spring Menu

Some birds eat worms too. They love spring rains that bring worms to the surface of the earth.

Summer Menu

In the summer, lots of birds eat insects. Some even sip the liquid nectar from flowers. A flower garden attracts lots of birds!

1. How is the heading of the last paragraph helpful?

2. Why do you think a bird's diet might change with the seasons?

3. What other animals might use their homes as sources of food? Make a list.

Try It!

Read a magazine or book about plants that eat animals or animals that eat plants.

Test-Taking Strategy: Identifying and Using Important Words

Pay attention to important words in directions and questions. These important words will help you find the correct answers.

Identifying and Using Important Words

The directions have important words. Each question has important words too. You have to listen to these words or read them carefully to answer the questions correctly.

> Look at the answers. Which word means the SAME as *large?*
> ○ big   ○ funny   ○ sad

The first answer is correct. *Big* means the SAME as *large.* Find the first answer, and point to the circle next to it.

Here is another question. Listen carefully.

Look at the answers. Which word means the OPPOSITE of *happy*?

○ big ○ funny ○ sad

The third answer is correct. *Sad* means the OPPOSITE of *happy*. To answer this question correctly, you had to pay attention to the word OPPOSITE. Find the third answer, and point to the circle next to it.

STOP

Test-Taking Practice

Read the story below. Then complete the test on the next page.

Wildflower Garden

Most gardens have flowers in rows. There is another kind of garden. It has many kinds of flowers. They are all mixed up. This is called a wildflower garden.

Making this kind of garden is easy. First you rake the ground. Next you throw the seeds onto the ground. Then you water the seeds and wait. In a few weeks, you will have pretty flowers!

Complete the test below.

Test Tip

Read each question carefully.

1. A wildflower garden is different because it

○ has no flowers.

○ has no rows.

○ has no seeds.

2. The story says that making a wildflower garden is

○ easy.

○ tiring.

○ silly.

3. Before you throw the seeds, you must

○ pick the flowers.

○ water the ground.

○ rake the ground.

STOP

283

Pronunciation Key

a as in **a**t

ā as in l**a**te

â as in c**a**re

ä as in f**a**ther

e as in s**e**t

ē as in m**e**

i as in **i**t

ī as in k**i**te

o as in **o**x

ō as in r**o**se

ô as in b**ou**ght and r**a**w

oi as in c**oi**n

o͞o as in b**oo**k

o͞o as in t**oo**

or as in f**or**m

ou as in **ou**t

u as in **u**p

ū as in **u**se

ûr as in t**ur**n, g**er**m, l**ear**n, f**ir**m, w**or**k

ə as in **a**bout, chick**e**n, penc**i**l, cann**o**n, circ**u**s

ch as in **ch**air

hw as in **wh**ich

ng as in ri**ng**

sh as in **sh**op

th as in **th**in

t͟h as in **th**ere

zh as in trea**s**ure

The mark (ˊ) is placed after a syllable with a heavy accent, as in **chicken** (**chik**ˊ ən).

The mark (ˏ) after a syllable shows a lighter accent, as in **disappear** (**dis**ˊ ə pērˊ).

Glossary

A

aside (ə sīd´) *adv.* To one side.

attracts (ə trakts´) *v.* Form of the verb **attract:** To draw attention to.

B

bean (bēn) *n.* A kind of seed that can be eaten as a vegetable.

bean

blade (blād) *n.* A thin leaf.

blocked (blokt) *v.* Past tense of **block:** To stop something.

blooming (blo͞om´ ing) *adj.* Flowering.

boggy (bog´ē) *adj.* Soft and watery.

bright (brīt) *adj.* Colorful.

buds (budz) *n.* Plural of **bud:** An unopened flower.

buds

Pronunciation Key: **a**t; l**ā**te; c**â**re; f**ä**ther; s**e**t; m**ē**; **i**t; k**ī**te; **o**x; r**ō**se; **ô** in b**ou**ght; c**oi**n; b**o͝o**k; t**o͞o**; f**or**m; **ou**t; **u**p; **ū**se; t**û**rn; **ə** sound in **a**bout, chick**e**n, penc**i**l, cann**o**n, circ**u**s; **ch**air; **hw** in **wh**ich; ri**ng**; **sh**op; **th**in; **th**ere; **zh** in trea**s**ure.

bush (bo͝osh) *n.* A small tree with many branches that is close to the ground.

C

crashed (krasht) *v.* Past tense of **crash:** To fall and hit the ground hard.

D

dashed (dasht) *v.* Past tense of **dash:** To run very fast for a short time.

depend (di pend´) *v.* To need or rely on.

dew (do͞o) *n.* Moisture from the air that forms drops on the grass.

dining car (dīn´ ing kär) *n.* A room on a train where meals are served and eaten.

dribbled (drib´ əld) *v.* Past tense of **dribble:** To move the ball along by bouncing or kicking it. A term used in soccer or basketball.

E

eggshells (eg´ shelz) *n.* Plural of **eggshell:** The hard skin or outer coating of an egg.

energy (en´ er jē) *n.* The strength to do something.

engine (en´ jin) *n.* A machine that pulls a railroad train.

engine

F

fine (fīn) *adj.* Very nice.

flicked (flikt) *v.* Past tense of **flick:** To strike or move lightly and quickly.

flower (flou´ ûr) *adj/n.* A colored blossom.

frightened (frī´ tənd) *adj.* Afraid; scared.

G

grinned (grind) *v.* Past tense of **grin:** To smile.

I

insects (in´ sekts) *n.* Plural of **insect:** A six-legged bug with a three-part body and no backbone.

insects

K

kite (kīt) *n.* A toy that flies in the sky on a long string.

Pronunciation Key: at; lāte; câre; fäther; set; mē; it; kīte; ox; rōse; ô in bought; coin; boŏk; toō; form; out; up; ūse; tûrn; ə sound in about, chicken, pencil, cannon, circus; chair; hw in which; ring; shop; thin; there; zh in treasure.

L

laughter (laf´ tər) *n.* The sound a person makes when something is funny.

liquid (lik´ wid) *n.* A waterlike substance.

logs (logz) *n.* Plural of **log:** A piece of a tree trunk.

M

meadow (med´ ō) *n.* A grassy field.

mountain (moun´ tən) *n.* A very large hill.

mountain

N

nectar (nek´ tər) *n.* Sugary fluid given off by plants and collected by bees to make honey.

noise (noiz) *n.* A loud sound.

P

pace (pās) *n.* The speed of walking or running.

pale (pāl) *adj.* Light in color.

perhaps (pər haps´) *adv.* Maybe.

petals (pet´ əlz) *n.* Plural of **petal:** the colored, leaf-shaped part of a flower.

petals

pistil (pis´ təl) *n.* The center of a flower.

pitcher (pich´ ər) *adj./ n.* A container used for pouring and holding liquids.

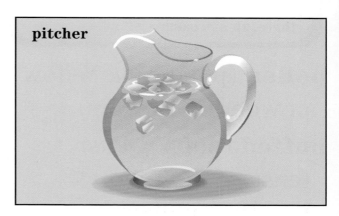

pitcher

plant (plant) *n.* A living thing that makes its own food and grows from the ground.

pleaded (plēd´ ed) *v.* Past tense of **plead:** To beg.

pods (podz) *n.* Plural of **pod:** A part of the plant that holds seeds.

poems (pō´ əmz) *n.* Plural of **poem:** A form of writing usually written in a rhyme.

pollen (pol´ ən) *n.* Yellow powder on flowers.

puffed (puft) *v.* Past tense of **puff:** To breathe quickly.

Q

quite (kwīt) *adv.* Very.

R

rather (ra/h´ ûr) *adv.* More gladly.

removes (ri mōōvz´) *v.* Form of the verb **remove:** To take away.

riddles (rid´ əlz) *n.* Plural of **riddle:** A question or problem that is hard to solve.

root (rōōt) *n.* The part of a plant that grows down into the ground.

root

rooted (rōōt´ed) *v.* Past tense of **root:** Fixed firmly.

S

saguaro (sə gwär´ō) *n.* A tall cactus that is found in the desert.

sailed (sāld) *v.* Past tense of **sail:** To move smoothly and quickly.

saved (sāvd) *v.* Past tense of **save:** To stop or block.

seeds (sēdz) *n.* Plural of **seed:** what a plant grows from.

seeds

senses (sens´ əz) *n.* Feelings.

shiny (shī´ nē) *adj.* Bright and sparkling.

shouted (shout´ ed) *v.* Past tense of **shout:** To call loudly.

shrub (shrub) *n.* A small tree or bush.

silky (sil´ kē) *adj.* Soft and smooth.

slippery (slip´ ûr ē) *adj.* Very smooth; wet or slimy.

soaks (sōks) *v.* Form of the verb **soak:** To get very wet.

soil (soil) *n.* The part of the ground where plants grow; dirt; earth.

spider (spī´ dər) *n.* A small animal with eight legs that spins webs to catch food.

spider

spines (spīnz) *n.* Plural of **spine:** A thorn; a sharp pointed tip on a plant or animal.

spread (spred) *v.* To open wide or stretch out.

spun (spun) *v.* Past tense of **spin:** To make a web.

stamens (stā´ mənz) *n.* Plural of **stamen:** Part of the flower that makes pollen.

stems (stemz) *n.* Plural of **stem:** The stalk of a flower or plant.

still (stil) *adj.* Not moving.

stomped (stompt) *v.* Past tense of **stomp:** To walk heavily; to stamp with one foot.

store (stor) *v.* To put away for the future.

T

thud (thud) *n.* A sound made when something heavy drops on the ground.

tight (tīt) *adv.* Held firmly; secure.

tips (tips) *n.* Plural of **tip:** The point or end.

tired (tīrd) *adv.* Sleepy.

tracks (traks) *n.* Plural of **track:** Where a train runs.

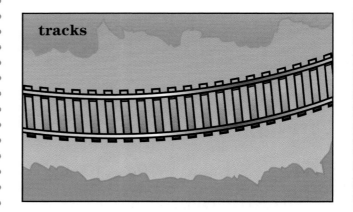

tracks

trapping (trap´ ing) *v.* Form of the verb **trap:** To allow entrance but no exit.

try (trī) *v.* To work at doing something better.

tucked (tukt) *v.* Past tense of **tuck:** To fold or push the ends of something into place.

vine (vīn) *n.* A plant that has a very long stem. A vine can grow along the ground or up a wall.

washed (wosht) *v.* Past tense of **wash:** To carry away by flowing water.

waterspout (wô´ tər spout) *n.* A pipe that catches roof water.

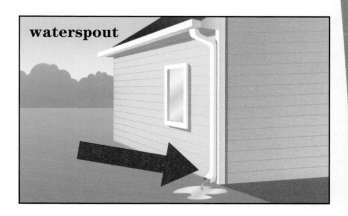

wetlands (wet´ landz) *n.* Plural of **wetland:** Land consisting of marshes and swamps.

wove (wōv) *v.* Past tense of **weave:** To turn and twist into a web.

yards (yärdz) *n.* Plural of **yard:** A place for railroad cars.